TUNISIA

THE ORIENT ON OUR DOORSTEP

WHITE STAR PUBLISHERS

Text
Paolo Rinaldi

Layout
Anna Galliani

Map
Cristina Franco

Translation
Barbara Fisher

Contents

1 *White walls and blue shutters are a characteristic sight all over Tunisia; the picture also shows, in the background, an elegant square tower, one of the many minarets of the* medina *of Tunis.*

2-3 *Right below the mountainous tip of Cap Bon are some interesting Roman caves, ancient quarries used to extract building materials; approximately 2 miles from the village of El Haouaria, they are reached from Kelibia or Nabeul. The road to the caves runs straight through the village and ends near the small* Café Les Grottes.

4-5 *The landscape of southern Tunisia is marked by date palms of which all parts are put to good use: the fruit is eaten, the leaves provide shelter and fencing, the trunk fuel. Palms are particularly plentiful and common in the oases, where they form large groves.*

6-7 *The picture shows a view of the Kroumirie region on the border with Algeria. The name originates from the first inhabitants, the brigand Kroumir tribes, whose raids and rebellions gave France the excuse to occupy Tunisia in 1881.*

8 *Marriage is still a major celebration, especially in the villages; in the towns customs tend to be more westernised, with private receptions held for close relations and best friends.*

9 *Arabesqued wrought-iron gates close the courtyard in front of the Bourguiba mausoleum; built in the Sixties and extended in 1978 it contains the mortal remains of the family of former president Habib Bourguiba, the man who led Tunisia towards independence.*

© 1998 White Star s.p.a.
Via C. Sassone, 22/24
13100 Vercelli, Italy
www.whitestar.it

New updated edition in 2007

ISBN: 978-88-544-0261-4

Reprints:
1 2 3 4 5 6   11 10 09 08 07

Colour separations by Graphic Service, Milan.
Printed in Singapore

SICILY

Malta

11 top right *The picture shows a typical view of southern Tunisia: a cluster of palm trees standing close to a water spring.*

11 centre left *The remains of the Capitol and the gate of Emperor Antoninus Pius lie at Sbeitla, the ancient Sufetula.*

11 centre right *The ribat, the fort, built in the 9th century, can be clearly distinguished from the top of the minaret of the Great Mosque of Sousse.*

11 bottom left *The small fishing port of Mahdia, about 35 miles from Sousse, takes on particularly charming appearance at dusk.*

12-13 *Popular traditions are still important on the island of Jerba and marriages are organised in great pomp with costumes and local participation.*

14-15 *The landscape of the coast of Tabarka, in northern Tunisia on the border with Algeria, is rugged and dramatic. Although the lovely natural port of the town was exploited by the Carthaginians, it really prospered under the Romans, who built the causeway that connects the small island in front of it with the mainland.*

16-17 *The white houses of Kelibia stand out on the other side of the small gulf; an important fishing centre with hotels and beaches, its picturesque port is dominated by a fort.*

Introduction

My memories of travel in Tunisia date only from the early Seventies but I have heard stories that go much farther back in time; I would treasure such memories as Tunisia has changed greatly and there is always the feeling of wonderful and unique experiences missed.

My first trip was by plane from Rome; we landed at the old El Aouina airport, a vaguely military-looking hangar flanked by a control tower. But my most vivid memories are of chaotic departures, everyone crowded around the only desk, in front of the only assistant, who would check the ticket thrust closest, ticking the name off a long list, containing far more names than the aeroplane could possibly hold. At passport control, the officials used the photograph to see which way up the document was to be held; even so they stamped the last page, which for them is the first.

The immediate impression from the plane was extraordinary: bare coast with a deep blue sea; you flew once over the salt lake of el Bahira, only to return for a second passage, lower down, in line with the runway. In summer the lake would be putrid and blood-red with fish secretions. Once out of the airport you quickly learned to buy a bunch of *fleurs de jasmine*; these were then worn behind the left ear, on the same side as the heart, but only by the men. Tunisia of the early Seventies was still a male universe.

I remember sea voyages too; cars loaded onto ferries sailing from Genoa or Palermo; early in the morning entering the golden calm of the Gulf of Tunis between the hill of Sidi Bou Said and the Kelibia peninsula, with Mount Bou Kornine, twin-peaked like the devil's horns. This was the same route taken centuries earlier, first by the Tyrian galleys, then the boats of Barca, the triremes of Scipio, the Turkish corsairs, the fleet of Charles V and the French steamboats. You disembarked almost in town but today the port is farther away. Then it was one great adventure, from the very first stop for petrol at a magnificent kiosk clad with Andalusian tiles – a sort of mini mosque complete with cupola and fake minaret.

In 1973-74 Boeings took the place of the Caravelles and the old airport went into retirement, not however without a big celebration one New Year's Eve. The new international airport of Carthage, repeatedly extended, was from the very beginning slightly pharaonic, with a dual staircase leading to departures. Tunisia was now taking hundreds of thousands of tourists in the few existing

hotels: the *Tunis Hilton*, with its annexe on the sea, the *Abou Nawas* in Gammarth, which also had the *Mégara*, or the *Hamilcar*, at the foot of the Sidi Bou Said hill, the *Jugurtha* in Sousse, the *Skanes* in Monastir, the *Oasis* in Gabès, the *Sahara Palace* in Nefta and the *Ulysses* in Jerba. These were big hotels and we preferred the *Dar Zarouk*, a former Bey residence, in Sidi Bou Said or the beautiful and luxurious *El Menzel* in Jerba, built with white blocks like the houses on the island. Without our own car, transfers around town were made in *petits taxis*, economical 4 horse-power cars or, for long distances, *louages*, the shared taxis found in all the Arab countries; these leave for a specific destination as soon as they are full – which means with at least two people more than the car can hold. The *Hotel du Lac* appeared towards the end of the Seventies, at the corner of Avenue Bourguiba and Avenue de la République; an inverted pyramid, it was a counter-attraction of the future to all the monuments of the past, which can be symbolised by the colosseum of El Jem.

In those years Tunisia turned modern. In Avenue Bourguiba, where the birds, hidden in the branches of the trees, chatter loudly at dusk and dawn, there are still octagonal newspaper kiosks, vendors of flowers and wedding garlands, of single cigarettes, a few shoeshine boys and a rare woman wrapped in a white veil. The *Africa Hotel* is a piece of high-rise New York, but just turn the corner from Place de l'Indépendence and you are in the rowdy Bab Souika square, a city within the city.

The asphalt has cancelled the traces of the Punic mercenaries, the Roman legions, the hordes of Vandals and the refined Byzantines, the Prophet's horsemen and the Spanish infantry, but Tunis, like most of north Africa, is made of Islam and Israel, of Malta, of Sicily and of Corsica. And before these it is made of Berbers. All the world has passed through and left something. Certain skylines resemble those of Syracuse and Messina; and Italian television has brought a third spoken language to Tunis and the northern part of the country: Italian, after the Arabic and French that are obligatory at school.

The Tunisians have for more than ten centuries been accustomed to contacts and exchanges with Europe, to the practice of hospitality and dialogue. So tolerant and so culturally advanced was Tunisia, that in 1956 a law was passed giving women equality and abolishing polygamy – a revolution for the Arab world. The *medina* of Tunis has lost its walls, knocked down in 1950; it is home to a cheerful, tenacious and indulgent people. The vendors used to be discreet, but now they are persistent. No smell of petrol penetrates to disturb the fragrance of mutton, jasmine and spices. The Arab cafés are tiled blue and green; the restaurants are tiny but serve excellent couscous, as do the luxury restaurants;

18 top   Tamerza is a splendid mountain oasis with an old abandoned village clinging to a rocky ridge. There is a hotel with restaurant and swimming pool above the gorge, through which runs the oued, *the river. This has three hot, warm and cold waterfalls one after the other. A short section of the railway line was recently reinstated at Tamerza, set amidst splendid gorges.*

18 bottom   The Tunisian landscape is dotted with whitewashed constructions – such as this at Degache – nearly always consisting of a square base topped with a dome. These are the tombs of famous people thought to be saints, marabouts, *the name also used for these mausoleums, which are places of worship. The doors are usually painted green, the colour of the Prophet.*

19 top *All over northern Tunisia, especially near the border with Algeria, the hills and mountains are covered with bushes and woods. These areas are visited only by hunters and archaeology enthusiasts and are where many of the remains of Roman towns have been found.*

19 bottom *The scenery along the jagged coasts of the north resembles that of southern Europe: plains farmed with cereals, large sandy beaches and olive groves. The views are often bucolic, dotted with farms – very distant one from the other – that also practise stockbreeding.*

the pastry shops display confections with unlikely colours; the interminable crowd will drag you into the remotest *souqs* filled with carpets, jewels, leather, brass, fabrics and spices. Familiarity is the rule and, having heard your friends, the vendors call you by name, offering you mint tea, not because they want to sell, but to get to know you, so that they are selling to a friend.

The city is growing and tourists rarely pass through Bab el Souika, where the grey and white houses start, where the workers, the tradesmen and the clerks sleep; beyond Bab el-Khadra and Belhaouane they demolish and rebuild in a blend of Latin and Arab, technical and manual, Islam and the West, with logic and improvisation.

Also in Tunisia poverty drives people to the cities; in the Eighties this phenomenon reached a climax in Tunis with the bidonvilles of Bergel, Melassine, Saida Manoubia, Sidi Bel Hassen, Gargouma and Sidi Fatallah, now converted to brick-built districts. But the Tunisian population has not stopped growing, despite the campaigns that promoted "no more than two children" and, if once the objective was to live in the capital, now those who have nothing, not even a job, dream of Italy.

This is one place that I remember has never changed in Tunis: the station of the legendary T.G.M., the little all-white train that connects Tunis with La Goulette and La Marsa. This light-rail train passes through the places where Tunisian history commenced, stopping at stations with names like Hamilcar, Hannibal, Carthage, Salammbô, as well as Présidence, where the Supreme Fighter, Habib Bourguiba, had the presidential residence built, alongside the remains of the Roman city. Now that the port of Carthage resembles a pond and all the rest has been reduced to ruin, you can only imagine the ships bearing amphoras, the priestess of Tanit, the young Romans in the Antonine baths, the head of Moloch, the elephants of Hamilcar. In order to see something of Carthage, a small Punic city, you have to cross the gulf and go to Kerkouane, on Cap Bon. Or you can visit the excavations around the cathedral.

The Berbers were there a long time ago. They were given their name by the Arabs, from the Latin *Barbari;* nomads and shepherds who had survived all the persecutions, they were already there when a queen called Dido arrived from afar; with an ox hide cut in narrow strips she founded an empire that would soon cross the seas and prosper through trade. Thus was born the Punic Libya that clashed with Rome in Sicily. The wars between the two powers lasted a hundred years. The *delenda Carthago* spoken by Cato caused the third Punic war, won by Scipio Aemilianus. Punic Libya ceased to exist and Roman Africa was born.

It was the time of the colony of Utica, with Jugurtha and the civil war between Caesar and

Pompey; although not until the peace of Augustus in the year 29 could Africa be said to be ruled by the Romans. Five centuries of domain followed, of roads and cities, of stones, columns, mosaics and aqueducts. Names such as Le Kef, Thuburbo Majus, Dougga, the ancient Thugga, commanding the Teboursouk plain, El Jem, the symbol of Roman pride, set like a precious stone in the middle of a steppe, with entertainment provided to the thousand shopkeepers that purchased the oil of the prosperous Thysdrus. To understand Rome, you must visit the Bardo museum in Tunis which conserves mosaics illustrating the arts and crafts of the colonists. Then came Christian Rome, in the fourth century, and as Rome declined in luxury and discord and the African settlers continued to produce wheat and oil, the Vandals were descending from the north via the Balearics. On 19th October 439, Genseric entered Carthage with 80,000 men and women. They were schismatic Catholics allied with Byzantium, but they too suffered revenge, a century later, when the Byzantines took over Carthage. Constantly at war with the Numidians, the wind of change was to blow from the east, a wind raised not far away that was destined to change the history of the world: in 647 the Arabs defeated the Byzantine army and in 670 Uqba Bin Nafi al-Fihri, the founder of Kairouan, arrived. It was the end of Africa and the birth of Ifriqiya.

Kairouan was the only city not already in existence and conquered, but completely founded by the Arabs out of nothing, fifty years after Egira, and it immediately became the centre of their empire. Seven trips to Kairouan equal one trip to Mecca. There is two days' gallop between one minaret and the other. From afar it looks like a mirage. It was the holy city and would continue to enchant even centuries later: in 1914 Paul Klee wrote in his diary: "The colour possesses me. There is no need to try to catch hold of it. It possesses me, I know." The Great Mosque of Kairouan was built with columns pillaged from ruins all over Tunisia, as if it were a museum to the victory. Kairouan looks in on itself, introverted; still today its *zaouia* (religious colleges) house young people unattuned to the West. Tunisia entered the modern world in 1957 when the Constitution sanctioned the lay government of Bourguiba; this was a dramatic time especially for Kairouan.

At the end of the 7th century all of Ifriqiya was Muslim; even the Berbers had converted. From that moment on its history was that of the Empire, battles between Fatimids and Omayyads, representatives of orthodoxy, while Ali became the martyr of the Shiites. History then became too complex to be told in a few lines. Much happened between then and 1048, when the emir of Tunis, El Moezz, declared independence both from Cairo and from Baghdad. The sultan of Cairo set the Huns of Africa, the Hillals, against him and, in the general

20 *Ksar Ouled Soultane is the stronghold of a nomad tribe of southern Tunisia and consists in two communicating courtyards, built at different times. Still used and inhabited by a few people, this* ksar *is exceptionally large, with* ghorfas *(granaries) on up to five storeys. It fills up now only on Fridays for prayers in the mosque.*

21 top *The villages on the Kerkennah archipelago, consisting of the two large islands of Gharbi (western) and Chergui (eastern) and a few islets, live on fishing. The two main islands, separated by a causeway built in Roman times, are linked to Sfax with frequent ferries used mainly to transport lorries loaded with palm fronds to the island; this raw material serves the fishermen to make traps that are laid on the sea bed to capture fish as the tide ebbs.*

21 bottom *Boats fitted with lateen sails and oars are a characteristic sight of the Kerkennah islands, 15 miles off the coast of Sfax.*

terror, the Normans and the Moroccan Almohads joined in; the latter entered Tunis in 1159 and installed the Hafsid dynasty. This ruled for three hundred years and returned the capital to that Mediterranean sea that had witnessed the birth of Carthage.

The Hafsids built the walls and the *souqs*, fortified the port and turned Tunis into a truly cosmopolitan capital. Africa and Europe were being mixed once more; from Spain came architects; from Marseilles and Venice came merchants; Jews and Levantines opened banks. Then, in the 16th century, the Hafsids allowed piracy to expand because they considered it to be an important kind of economic activity. The Berber corsairs roved the Mediterranean plundering ships, goods and slaves. The dynasty resisted all attacks but not the joint efforts of the Turks and Spanish, the Barbarossa brothers, on the one hand, and Charles V, on the other. In 1534 Khair-ed-Din Barbarossa seized Tunis, but a year later, an armada of 400 ships led by the king in person imposed a Spanish protectorate on Tunisia which lasted 35 years. More corsairs appeared on the scene, at the service of the Sublime Porte: Draghut of Tripoli and the Calabrian Ali the Renegade who, paid by the Turks, managed to occupy Tunis in 1569. Power thus passed to the Janissary dynasty, until 1612 when the Bey dynasty was founded.

The Turkish empire, after the death of Suleiman the Magnificent, was going through a crisis and the Bey monarchy ruled until 1881, the year when the French protectorate was established. In the meantime, the Beys had perfected the art of piracy; as still happens today they acquired the weapons and raw materials for their ships in Europe. Nothing ever really changes. The galley crews were recruited in Malta and Piraeus, at Leghorn, Marseilles and Barcelona. The Christian prisoners were freed at a dear price, but many had no one that could pay and they converted, practising in Tunis the trade they had learnt at home. France, Spain, Florence and Malta needed Turkish slaves for their ships and it became one large exchange, governed by agreements and treaties, in which France came out better than other nations. In 1685 Colbert drew up a treaty of mutual assistance with the Tunisia of the Beys, opening a *funduk* (trading port) in Tunis that quickly became the most important of all.

In 1811 the Janissary corps was broken up. Africa was no longer a rival but a prey of the European powers, who decided to put an end to piracy. None of the Beys of Tunis came through the State's vicissitudes well. France and England, more than others, were looking for new places to exploit. France was already in Algeria with greedy ambition; the Beys found themselves in huge debt; Italy also had intentions. The English feared them, the Germans were in agreement; there was the pretext of the Kroumir forays and France invaded Tunisia, establishing a protectorate which was oppressive, morally unjust and deplorable, although in the long run positive for a brutal reawakening on the part of the upper Tunisian bourgeoisie.

The history of colonialism in Tunisia differs little from the stories we know, but the fight for liberation worked by the Neo-Destour party, led by a lawyer called Habib Bourguiba, was less cruel than others, such as that of Algeria, even though Tunisia did suffer sieges, repression, deaths and strikes in the mines with more deaths. With Morocco in revolt and the start of the war in Algeria, France was increasingly inclined to give in: 1954 saw the right to internal autonomy, and independence came on 20th March 1956. The Neo-Destour party – the name means constitution – had won. For Habib Bourguiba this marked the start of new problems, similar to those faced by Mohammed V and Nasser: all the contradictions of Arab nationalism, never resolved, never appeased, and so tragically present today in other countries. In 1957 the monarchy was abolished and Habib Bourguiba elected president of the Republic. In 1987, Zinelabidine Ben Ali became the second President of Tunisia. The rest is recent history, no less complex but perhaps better known.

Tunisia could be defined a country full of charm, but there are a thousand other definitions, one for each of its many faces. The beautiful scenery, the courteous people, their tenacious character, the air you breathe, the young people's enthusiasm, the Berber pride, the awareness of being a People and a Nation. Tunis is an enchanting city, no longer quietly cunning as it appeared in the past, but alive and ready to take initiatives of international importance. With its two million inhabitants, it is once more the most cosmopolitan city in the Maghreb. Just a few kilometres away beyond the places of its now silent past, on a steep hill above the sea, stands the loveliest village in the world, the delightful Sidi Bou Said, blue and white: blue as only the Tunisian sky can be, white as the sea foam that breaks on the rocks.

The coast to the north, towards Gammarth, proceeds unobtrusively with villas, luxury hotels and restaurants, patronised by everybody who is anybody in Tunis. All the coast is lined with holiday villages, unrecognisable for those who knew it some years ago. But many roads lead to Bizerte and Tabarka, on the border with Algeria; the landscape is very Mediterranean even on the inland plains, with rocky coasts that impose long detours amidst wheat fields and vineyards, marked by the presence of European-style farms; the sea close to Bizerte has a rural flavour, behind the headland that protects the bay to the east. Occupied by the French for nearly a

22-23 *The women of the island of Jerba wear the traditional veil on their heads and a straw hat to protect them from the wind that blows in all seasons, cool in summer, cold in winter. The island has changed greatly in recent years under the onslaught of mass tourism, with dozens of hotels and holiday villages being built. The capital Houmt Suq, originally a village, has now become a town with a souq; particularly rich and interesting, this branches out in a crowded tangle of shops, small squares and streets, often covered. The island's economy is still partly bound to agriculture and the manufacture of pottery, practised mostly in the village of Guellala where even the streets are in* opus signinum *(fragments of terracotta); the houses remain hidden behind kilns and mounds of earthenware debris and fragments. Jerba is the mythical land of the Lotus-Eaters* where Ulysses was held up on his way home after the end of the Trojan War by a people living in indolent forgetfulness, drugged by a legendary honey-fruit. Life is still sweet on the island of Jerba even just for a holiday, thanks to the temperate climate, beautiful scenery, the lovely square, white houses called* menzels, *courteous inhabitants and good cuisine. There are more than 200 mosques, all constructed using the basic combination of primary geometric volumes – cubes, prisms, cylinders and spheres. Since the time of the destruction of the temple of Solomon, the island has had a Hebrew community, living in the villages of Hara Kabira and Hara Saghira. The Ghriba synagogue – the name means Marvellous – conserves one of the oldest known* torah *(books of the law) in an Oriental setting.*

hundred years, Bizerte has inherited the spirit and the feel of that country, with its wide tree-lined avenues leading to an old canal port teeming with fishing boats. The *kasbah* presents all the subjects of the late 19th-century Orientalist painters, including the characteristic colours – fantastic when put together – of ochre and light blue.

As you descend south from Tunis you rediscover the charm of the gulf in the curve of the bay of Hammamet, and even sooner in the rolling hills of the Kelibia peninsula, mildly Sicilian in appearance, the crops separated by prickly-pear cactus hedges, in the dainty villages so reminiscent of Andalusia: Dar Chaabane, Beni Khiar, surrounded by olive and citrus groves, tomatoes, tobacco and peppers, put out to dry in summer, as in Italy, on the walls of the houses. There are large farming towns and scattered peasants' houses, while at Kelibia the coast becomes rugged. Kerkouane is the only Punic town uncovered by the archaeologists, with its tanks for the farming of murex (a type of mollusc), used to produce a purple dye. At Ghar el Kebir are the large Roman quarries that provided the stone for, among other buildings, the Colosseum of El Jem. Farther south, off the coast of Sidi Daoud is the island of Zembra. Then comes Nabeul, the leading pottery-producing centre (along with Jerba) as well as being a centre for perfume essences distilled from flowers, silk or silver yarn embroidery, wrought-iron and chased brass. The kilns fill the air with the fragrant smell of olive branches, dry palms and esparto grass, used when baking the pots: both the yellow and green enamelled ones, which are traditional, and all the pottery, artistic and commercial, that is seen displayed in Tunisian markets.

From Nabeul the coast is one long row of tourist amenities and facilities as far as Hammamet, a symbol of the growth of mass tourism in Tunisia and beyond. But the sand is fine, the sea clean and blue, the hotels low-built and unoppressive and the old city has not lost its quiet charm and a socially attractive environment, with its tiny well-preserved *kasbah*.

To descend south from Tunis, you may choose to take the road to Zaghouan that allows a visit to Thuburbo Majus and to arrive directly in Kairouan. At Zaghouan there are the springs that used to and indeed still do supply Tunis (the remains of the aqueduct can be seen along the road) and a famous monument called the *Temple des Eaux*, a large fountain at the base of the mountain.

The scenery changes: Sahel, literally shore, starts south of Hammamet; at Kairouan the steppe begins. This has always been a land of nomad shepherds, while olives were gathered in Sahel. Today the nomads have nearly all settled, and even practise some form of farming; on the coast a greater source of income has been developed: tourism. The coast does still present some virgin territory, where the *sebkhas* are situated for example; these are hollows that fill

24-25 *The Portico of the Petronii gymnasium precedes the Summer baths, the most sumptuous of the two buildings (the other being the Winter baths) which, together with the market, complete the public amenities in the Thuburbo Majus town centre, 35 miles* or so from Tunis. Probably of Berber origin, Thuburbo Majus was occupied by the Romans after the defeat of Carthage and achieved considerable economic prosperity, enabling it become first a Roman municipium *and then a colony.*

with salt water in winter and are common in the Enfidaville area. The roads follow the routes of the ancient *pistes*, such as that leading to Sousse, the third largest city in Tunisia, arisen on the site of the former colony of Hadrumète. Repeatedly destroyed, even by the Arabs who founded Kairouan, it owes its rebirth to the Aghlabids. The *medina* is its most interesting part, with a lovely restored Great Mosque in ancient style and with late additions. The other important monument in Sousse is the *ribat*, a fortified-monastery serving to protect the inhabitants, built in stages at various times. The kasbah is reached by passing through colourful *souqs*. The new building housing the museum was constructed to house magnificent mosaics and the finds of the *tophet* (citadel) of Punic Hadrumète.

There is no break between Sousse, Skanès and Monastir: all salt lakes, palm groves and rows of hotels, but the approach to Monastir brings the surprise view of the fortress incorporating the *ribat*. Unfortunately, it then emerges that part of the *medina* was destroyed to make way for film sets, including a Greek temple, now impossible to shift. No matter, the fortress is beautiful, with many alterations having been made to the original *ribat* founded in 796. *Son et Lumière* shows are held in the two courtyards, but it deserves a proper visit with a climb up to the top of the *nador*, the tower, which affords splendid views of the whole; the different areas can be identified with the help of a plan or a guide. A small manuscript museum has been set up inside the prayer room.

The road that continues southwards crosses the town of Moknine, famous for filigree jewellery and a *cloisonné* enamel, also called Moknine. A small museum explains its origin and recently-made jewellery is found in nearly all the shops. Mahdia took its name from El Mahdi ('one who is guided' to convert the world to Islam), a self-proclaimed caliph; he rose against the Aghlabids and founded the Fatimid dynasty, who later moved their capital to Cairo. There are at least two buildings of major importance here, both military: the Skifa el-Kahla and the Borj el-Kebir; the former is an imposing gate in the town walls and the latter a quadrangular fortress built by the Turks. The Great Mosque, founded by El Mahdi in the 10th century, was rebuilt thirty years ago.

Farther south, amidst olive groves, some recently established, is the second-largest city in Tunisia, Sfax; it has an important trading port, a large industrial area and a sizeable fishing fleet. Boats leave from the port for the Kerkennah islands. But first take a look at the *medina* which has turned into an immense *souq*, perhaps one of the most interesting in Tunisia for the quantity of products on offer, not for the tourists, but for domestic demand.

The Kerkennah islands are a hour by ferry from the port of Sfax and rise just above the water; the highest point is 40 feet and there are many periodically submerged *sebkhas*. The islands have few hotels, little tourism and not many inhabitants, but they are beautiful, with a Polynesian appearance and the relaxed pace of an economy based on farming and fishing, the latter practised in a strange and archaic manner. The sea bed is flat, but the tide rises considerably; the islands abound with palm trees and the fronds are used to build dams, called *cherfiyah*, complete with traps into which the fish swim when the tide is ebbing. Octopus is also caught in a novel manner, by lowering pots into the sea and imprisoning the creatures.

Back on the mainland there are eucalyptus trees and steppe on the one side and sea on the other; the scenery changes as you approach the splendid oasis of Gabès, a palm oasis, dark in outline and jagged. You cross the oasis to enter the town; it has an ancient history but lacks monuments or relics, a middle-class countenance with no specific traits, a modern appearance of building development along 12 miles of coastline, not much tourism, but the lovely Jara *souq* in a colonial building and, above all, a marine oasis which provides an interesting walk.

The approach to the island of Jerba is striking: you cross a plateau called Jorf, which means rock; the road runs through olive groves but suddenly comes within sight of a lovely red rock where the land finishes in the sea. Today the ferries are modern and carry many cars, but there used to be only a barge that went to and fro, carrying just two cars at a time, a veritable boat of Charon so slow that you thought you would never land at the Adjim pier; the island, like a mirage in the distance, seemed to drift away and, at the same time, became ever more real and beautiful, if less mysterious. Jerba really was for years an enchanted island; it still is, though it has lost a little of the charm, the adventure of days past is no more and there is no longer the thrill of difference, difference from all, from Tunisia itself. It remains beautiful with lovely *menzel* architecture, square white houses that form indistinct villages, crops, palm trees, the olive trees, sudden sand dunes, cutting wind, and an incredible silence. The only true town is Houmt Suq, with lovely mosques and old *funduks* turned into charming hotels, cafés where they smoke the *narghilé* (long pipe with aromatic water in it), restaurants that serve excellent fish, and a *souq*, rich and for the most part still authentic.

From Jerba you can descend along a deserted coast to the border with Libya, but most prefer to visit Medenine and its *ksar* – a fortified village with splendid *ghorfas* (granaries), their entrances opened in the fired clay. There used to be 25 courtyards with more than 6,000 *ghorfas*; regrettably all were destroyed in 1962 save two courtyards to make way for new constructions in a desert area. Medenine is to some extent the

26 *Spices of all kinds and colours are much used in Tunisian cuisine to flavour food. Tunisian cuisine is not always hot and, despite the cliché, is not just couscous; it has the largest variety of dishes in north Africa. Couscous is the national speciality, popular also in Algeria, Morocco and Trapani, in Sicily. There are 50 or so recipes but all are based on semolina cooked in the steam of a soup, boiled vegetables or meat, fish or other. The couscous is then served with the foods used to cook it. Tunisian cuisine includes extraordinary dishes such as* tajine, *a quiche of meat, onions, eggs and cheese;* mouloukhia, *meat cooked with a highly fragrant blend of spices;* shakshuka, *a pepper stew with eggs;* brik, *filled flaky pastry fried; and* mechouia, *grilled meats of all kinds.*

27 top *The archivolt of a door in perforated white marble; here, as is often the case, it is surrounded by a black and white banded arch.*

27 bottom *The picture shows characteristic Berber jewellery in silver with silver-strand applications and decorations of red coral from the coasts of northern Tunisia. This jewellery tells much of Berber culture and art although the nomads or even the now-settled populations have never produced their own jewellery. It has always been designed and handmade for them by craftsmen belonging to the Hebrew communities, the only ones skilled in of beating, welding and casting silver leaf.*

centre of the great Tunisian south.

Farther south is the pre-desertic steppe, the realm of the nomads. Foum Tataouine, home of the Foreign Legion's gaol, and where the Neo-Destour leaders were exiled, has regained a normal appearance. The Berber women dress in cotton pretending they still cover their faces with a veil; weekly markets draw Berbers and bedouins to buy hand-spun wool, camel-hide shoes with rubber-tyre soles, the long strips used to make bedouin tents, carpets of all sorts, shawls and jewellery. Returning northwards, Gabès can be used as a base for a visit to parts of south-east Tunisia, such as the farming and handicraft village of Chenini; the village of Oudref that produces carpets to a design that originated in Tripoli, Libya; Matmata, the most famous of the underground troglodyte villages (although the most beautiful *ghorfas* are at Hadej and Téchine, not far away).

From the sea, from Gabès, you enter the desert, surrounded by *chotts* (salt lakes), perhaps crossing tiny oases, entering western-movie settings to climb up the mountain that leads down into the oasis of Kebili, encircled by the first sands of the Grand Erg (Desert) Oriental; as you advance this increasingly adopts the traditional form of dunes in invisible movement, until you reach Douz, famous for its camel market and palm oases that produce the *deglet nour*, the finger of light dates, sweet and as transparent as alabaster. The blue of the north has disappeared: here all is ochre. The harsher the scenery becomes, the more intense become the colours of the women's clothes and the more abundant and heavy their jewellery.

With a cross-country vehicle and a good supply of food and petrol you can arrive at Ksar Ghilene, passing through Bir Soltane. From Kebili you can go to Tozeur and expect some mirages: you drive for 30 miles in the flat expanse of the *chott* where anything may appear, to arrive at the Grand Erg Oriental, where the largest oasis is that of Tozeur. This marvellous village offers extraordinary examples of a highly refined urban Berber architecture, as can also be seen in the nearby Nefta with its Corbeille, oasis springs that maintain more than 350,000 palm trees.

On the mountains, towards Midès and the Tunisian border, stand the mountain oases of Tamerza and Chebika, nestled on the side of stunning canyons. But it is time to travel north again crossing the Metlaoui area, with its phosphate train that carried only fourth-class passengers, and then Gafsa to visit El Jem and the monumental amphitheatre, a massive presence in the centre of a town made up of modest dwellings. The last stop on this journey completes the circle of foundation and conquest, religion and fanaticism, tradition and modernity: the holy city of Kairouan, built on the site of a spring of water.

28-29 The white mosque of the village of Le Kef, perched on the side of a hill, is dominated by the massive profile of a kasbah, *with gates and walls dating from various periods. There is also a Turkish mosque inside, partially built in 1679 by Mohammed Bey with materials taken from ancient Roman and Byzantine monuments. Le Kef is on the road to the north coast, close to the Roman ruins of Maktar and Medeina.*

30-31 Not quite as large as the Colosseum in Rome, the amphiteatre in El Jem does have the same characteristics and is equally impressive. El Jem is in central Tunisia, close to Kairouan; the amphitheatre was built in AD 328 by Gordian, when he was made emperor. It was greatly damaged in 1695 when a group of dissidents took refuge inside and part of it was blown away to flush them out. Although later used as a quarry for materials, the monument is well preserved thanks to the extensive (clearly visible) restoration work done.

32-33 The modern mausoleum of Habib Bourguiba, first president of the Tunisian Republic, was erected at Monastir, his birthplace.

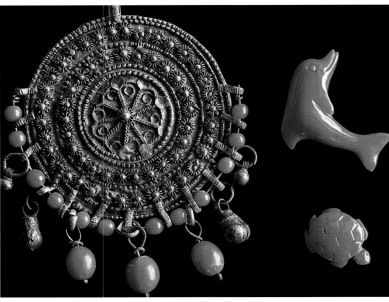

From the Mediterranean to the Sahara

34 top *The waters of the Mediterranean lap the dark and deserted north coast of Tunisia, close to Tabarka, born with the expansion of the town founded by the French in 1881. Some buildings have maintained the characteristic* fin du siècle *atmosphere.*

34 bottom *The Tunisian landscape is not always as barren as might be imagined. Vast areas have not yet been deforested, especially on the mountain slopes near the border with Algeria.*

35 *These palm trees in an oasis in southern Tunisia have been chosen as the ideal surroundings for the tomb of a* marabout *(holy man, considered a saint).*

Rocks fashioned by the waves

36-37 The north Mediterranean coast of Tunisia is rocky and inaccessible with picturesque cliffs and an often raging sea – ideal for underwater fishing enthusiasts. The town of Tabarka, almost 125 miles from Tunis, was a Phoenician trading colony and a Roman port. Later, it became a major coral-fishing centre. This activity was the prerogative of the Genoese Lomellini family, based on the island opposite the port of Tabarka. In 1741 the Bey of Tunis decided to occupy it and take the Genoese inhabitants prisoners; ransom was paid by Carlo Emanuele II of Savoy and they were transferred to the Sardinian island of San Pietro, where they founded the town of Carloforte. The bare little island opposite Tabarka conserves the ruins of a fortress built by the Genoese in the 16th century.

38-39 *The town of Korbous, 30 miles or so from Tunis, on the south coast, lies in a picturesque position and benefits from natural radioactive water springs that reach temperatures of up to 60°C. This is one of the best-known hydrothermal centres in Tunisia, patronised also by the Romans who had established a spa here called* Acquae Calidae Capitanae. *The modern spa building has a minaret and a crenellated terrace.*

39 left *As well as the spa that made it famous in Roman times and which remains a great tourist attraction (the sulphurous vapours apparently cure digestive and liver deficiencies, rheumatism, obesity, skin complaints and even some forms of sterility), Korbous can boast splendid natural scenery and a crystal-clear sea.*

39 right *Terracotta jugs and fishing boats used to represent the main economical resource of the island of Jerba, together with agriculture. Now times have changed and the principal source of income is that produced by the rapidly growing tourist industry.*

40 Carthage, just a few miles from Tunis and the capital of a great empire in the ancient world, is now a pleasant suburb of the capital overlooking the Gulf of Tunis, with views of the mountains on the Kelibia peninsula. Carthage was founded in 814 BC by the Phoenicians of Tyre. Later it fought for possession of Sicily with the Greek colony of Syracuse and with Rome, which destroyed it in 126 BC.

41 Of the ancient Carthage remain traces of the two ports, the trading one, an elongated rectangle, and the military one in a ring around the island that housed the arsenals. Today, as the picture shows, they are no longer connected to each other and, partially silted up, are hard to distinguish. The Tophet is fascinating; this is the cemetery where apparently the Phoenicians buried the new-born babies

sacrificed to the cult of the goddess Tanit. On the hill, the National Museum of Carthage exhibits all the finds made during excavations conducted in the area. The largest remains of Roman Carthage are the Antonine baths, a short distance from Carthage towards Sidi Bou Said. Much of their charm lies in the fact that they are situated on the waterfront.

Oases and deserts

42 top Close to Douz, in the desert, the springs are mainly freshwater but sometimes salt water gathers to form large lakes as in the case of Chott-el-Jerid, which stretches from north of Douz to Tozeur.

42 bottom Camels are the ships of the desert, the animals best-loved by the nomads for whom they provide a means of transport, milk, meat and hides. They are given countless names: indeed only Allah has more.

42-43 Occasional palm trees dot the south Tunisian landscape where the desert commences; camel caravans in movement are also a rare sight now. Where there are solitary palm trees there is water and often an oasis nearby, in this case that of Douz; this village has in recent years become a pleasant "alternative" attraction to Tozeur and Nefta, besieged by hordes of tourists.

43 The region of Douz is dominated by the extraordinary presence of sand dunes, their shape changing imperceptibly but continually with the wind.

44 top left *The oasis of Ksar Ghilane lies on the* piste *that descends from Gabès into the Tunisian Sahara, a mile or so past the monument to the Leclerc column. The gigantic tamarisks of the Sahara shade the spring which reduces to a trickle and then disappears in the dunes. The ksar (literally "fortified village") is just over a mile away although it is really a Roman fort of the* limes tripolitanus, *used for many years by the French army.*

44 top right *Just like the camels, palms have many names in the Berber tongue, as many as there are species. They are beautiful trees and the sight from above can be moving. An Arab proverb says there is no point in going to heaven unless it has palm oases.*

44 left *The old part of Gafsa conserves the characteristic appearance of Berber villages; the remainder is modern and bears the mark of a transformation based on European models. At the heart of the town are the* kasbah *and Roman pools, surrounded by high walls.*

44 bottom right *Gafsa has a rich supply of springs which form two main pools, dug into the rock by the Romans. The children of Gafsa dive in from the walls around, up to 30 feet high, and collect the coins thrown in by tourists.*

45 *The oasis of Gafsa is one of the loveliest in all Tunisia. It starts close to the* kasbah *and is extremely fertile with at least 100,000 date palms. There are also oranges, lemons, apricots and pomegranates; vine-shoots entwine the palm trunks. On the edge of the oasis are olive groves and clumps of cactus, used all over Tunisia for fencing.*

46-47 *Numerous oases have been created ex novo or artificially extended by the Tunisian government; the picture shows a typical mountain oasis close to the Grand Erg Oriental.*

The sign
of man

48 top left *The oasis of Seldja stands in a gorge along the road between Gafsa and Tozeur, beside a mountain eroded by the wind; thus transformed it looks like a natural fortress with steep, inaccessible walls.*

48 bottom left *The Ksar Ouled Soultane is one of the largest and best preserved ksour in southern Tunisia; it has hundreds of ghorfas, windowless rooms used as granaries by the nomad peoples. The ghorfas are stacked one on top of the other, sometimes reaching up to five storeys; access is via external stone steps in the wall.*

48 top right *Part of the Gafsa fortress, built in 1434 and devastated by an explosion in 1943, is still well preserved; the Law Courts were built in the void created by the explosion.*

48 bottom right *Matmata is a mountain oasis made up of two villages on a plateau almost completely devoid of vegetation. The old village is situated on two rocky peaks that dominate the landscape. The so-called new part consists of troglodyte dwellings dug into the walls of circular or polygonal wells having a diameter of 40 feet or so and as deep. Often on two levels, the rooms provide living and storage space and are connected to each other by tunnels.*

49 *A white-painted mosque occupies a narrow saddle close to Chenini. Perched on the top of a mountain, the village consists of a series of ghorfas, preceded by a closed courtyard and set in a spectacular natural amphitheatre.*

50 *The old* ksar *of Medenine stands in a huge square overlooked by ancient* ghorfas; *like beehives with stacked rows of narrow cells, they were originally used by the Bedouins as food stores but later also as dwellings. The only access to the cells is via primitive external steps.*

50-51 *Guermessa is a fortified Berber village reached from Chenini. Various levels of troglodyte dwellings have been created in this harsh, mountain landscape.*

52-53 *The mountains north of Nefta and Tozeur present splendid scenery; one example is this canyon a few miles long near the oasis of Tamerza, close to the Algerian border. The rocks here contain fossil shells and fish that the children sell to visitors for a few pence.*

53 *The small white mosque of Douiret is perched on a rocky face on top of which a* kalaa *was built in the 15th century; this fortress, served by a maze of passages, allowed the population to live permanently in the* ghorfas, *dug into the mountain. The settlement was abandoned only recently.*

All the green of the countryside

54-55 *Along the road that descends south from Tabarka and Suq el-Arba towards Gafsa is the Le Kef region, mountainous and covered with vegetation. The village of Le Kef, set on the side of a hill, is particularly pleasant in summer when the climate is cool; in winter the temperature falls considerably and it usually snows. Founded by the Phoenicians, Le Kef became the Roman colony of Sicca Veneria under Augustus and enjoyed a certain prosperity.*

55 top and centre *The whole Haidra area is cultivated, as are other parts of northern Tunisia, but the total yield of cereals, wheat and barley fails to meet the needs of the people and must be supplemented with imports. Cattle-breeding has also been developed in these northern regions.*

55 bottom *Travelling from north to south, past the Kroumir, you encounter an alternation of fertile plains and barren hills and small white houses interrupt a landscape dotted either with pine trees and cork oaks or with prickly-pear cactus.*

56 top *Olives and vines cover the gentle hillside landscape of El Alia, along the road between Bizerte and Raf Raf.*

56 centre *Bucolic scenes are no rare sight in the Maktar countryside, where the inhabitants farm cereals and breed animals.*

56 bottom *Sometimes, in the lushest parts of Tunisia, you come across fields of esparto, a grass exported for paper-making. This product is then collected at Thala, halfway between Le Kef and Kasserine.*

56-57 *Inhabited since ancient times, Maktar is a large farming village developed by the French from the end of the 19th century onwards; this was the start of their domination and more or less when the archaeological excavations, that now make it one of the most interesting areas in northern Tunisia, began.*

Ancient cities look to the future

58 top *The town of Mahdia was already inhabited in Phoenician and Roman times but owes its present appearance to the first Fatimid caliph, Obeid Allah al-Mahdi, who transferred the capital here from Kairouan in 912. He gave the name to the town which acquired some importance because of its strategic position, also in later centuries as a fortress first Arab, then Norman and Spanish. A huge wall, 32 feet thick, was constructed to defend the town. The entrance to the medina is through Skifa el-Kahla, the Dark Passage, an opening in the wall with iron gates that could be lowered.*

58 bottom *The picture shows a beautiful view of Zaghouan: to the fore is a mosque with an exposed-brick cupola, in the background square, white houses. The town is located at the foot of the jebel (mountain) of the same name from which flow the springs of the oued, the river of Tunis; these waters used to be carried to Carthage by a great Roman aqueduct 56 miles long and with bridges up to 65 feet high. Also linked to the spring is the Temple des Eaux, a fountain built in the time of Hadrian at the bottom of a rocky crag.*

59 *The village of Sidi Bou Said stands on the northern tip that closes the Gulf of Tunis. It is all blue and white, only the doors of the mosque being green, the colour of the Prophet. Since 1915 a strict municipal regulation has banned any changes to the external structure of the houses; the sale of alcohol is also forbidden and only permitted outside the village. Many foreigners have permanent homes here.*

Tunis, the gateway to Africa

60 top *The Porte de France marks the boundary between the new town and the* medina. *In Arabic it is called Bab el-Bahr, the "gate of the sea"; it stands alone because the walls were demolished in 1950. On one side starts Avenue de France, continuing with Avenue Habib Bourguiba, on the other is the entrance to the* medina, *along the street that rises towards the Great Mosque.*

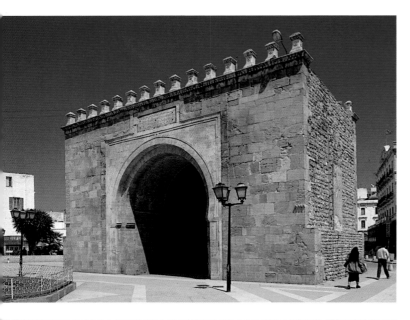

60 bottom *The Mosque of Sidi Mahres is the only one in Tunis to have domes similar to certain Turkish mosques; it is dedicated to the man considered the patron saint of Tunis, who lived in the mid-10th century.*

60-61 *The courtyard of the Great Mosque Ez Zitouna of Tunis, built in the centre of the* medina, *is seen from the top of the minaret. Tunis is one of the most ancient Mediterranean cities, a capital under the Aghlabids and then under the Hafsids, when the* souqs *and most of the mosques were built.*

61 top *The slender Harrouda Pasha minaret rises in the blue sky flanked by the flag of the Tunisian Republic.*

61 bottom *The cathedral of Saint Louis was built by the French in 1882 opposite the municipal theatre. It is dedicated to Louis IX, king of France and saint who in 1270 besieged Tunis in vain.*

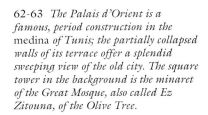

62-63 *The Palais d'Orient is a famous, period construction in the medina of Tunis; the partially collapsed walls of its terrace offer a splendid sweeping view of the old city. The square tower in the background is the minaret of the Great Mosque, also called Ez Zitouna, of the Olive Tree.*

62 bottom right *Colour becomes very important in a monotonous landscape such as that of semi-barren Tunisia; some elegant mansions in the capital feature deep blue windows and doors with arches painted in black and white bands standing out against green and yellow walls; the handles and door knockers are always black.*

62 top left *Many walls in the rooms of the Palais d'Orient are lined with ceramic tiles portraying stories and legends of the Arab world.*

62 top right *One of the great wonders of the medina of Tunis is the wealth of architectural detail, especially on the doorways, framed with geometric motifs enriched with large nails and moulding of various dimensions.*

64-65 *The main thoroughfare that is the backbone of the new city runs from the Porte de France towards the port, in the opposite direction to the medina; it was built in part by the French in European style with large department stores, luxury hotels, Western-type shops, restaurants and cafés with street tables, including the highly popular* Café de Paris. *The Place de l'Indépendence is almost at the end of Avenue Habib Bourguiba.*

65 left *Of fairly recent construction, this monument dedicated to the Independence has divided the population, some being still closely bound to more traditional images. The regime instead feels the need to assert itself with bold, modern works of engineering.*

65 top right *The aerial view of Avenue Habib Bourguiba is impressive, less for the architecture than for the extraordinary number of trees. At dusk the chirping of the birds that nest here is so loud that all normal conversation is impossible.*

65 centre right *Other monuments and large clocks dear to colonial tastes break up the long pedestrian promenade in the centre of Avenue Bourguiba, always very busy especially in the evening.*

65 bottom right *Tunis is a modern city in many senses, not least in the habits of the young people, totally European both in dress and everyday conduct.*

Ancient fortresses

66 top *The rocky island opposite Tabarka is crowned by a lovely fort built by the Genoese in 1540, when the island was given to the Lomellini family in exchange for the freedom of the corsair Dragut.*

66 bottom *Tabarka, on the north coast of Tunisia, near the border with Algeria, is the ancient Thabraka, founded by the Phoenicians. It also prospered under the Roman empire thanks to its port, used to export marble and minerals.*

67 top *The town of Tabarka played a leading role in the last World War, opposing the advance of the Italo-German troops who were trying to enter Algeria. Habib Bourguiba and his staff were exiled here for two months in 1952.*

67 bottom *Kelibia was born on the site of the ancient Clupea, founded by Agathocles on the coast of Cap Bon, then conquered by Regulus and destroyed by Scipio. It has a lovely fort at the top of a hill 500 feet high and dating from the 6th century with square towers and deep reservoirs. It has of course been much tampered with over the years but the exterior is still well preserved.*

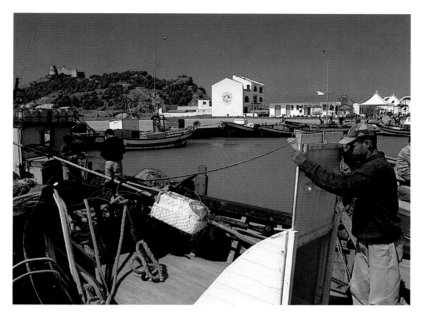

Bizerte, the French citadel

68 top *Some parts of old Bizerte are typically Mediterranean, very similar to villages in Corsica or Sardinia, also influenced by the Moors (who settled in the Andalusian quarter when expelled from Spain in 1492) and the Spanish of Charles V.*

68 bottom *Old Bizerte was a provincial town extending between the sea and a lake, with a massive* kasbah *and a Spanish fort, rich in atmosphere. Today it is a modern town, somewhat*

anonymous but very much alive. The destruction worked by the Second World War and the demolition required for its reconstruction have completely changed its appearance. Nonetheless the old Bizerte deserves a visit for what remains of the port, canal and fortifications.

68-69 *The old port of Bizerte still resembles a delightful painting with its two-storey houses all different heights, behind the picturesque fishing boats.*

Le Kef, the capital of the west

70 top *The old town of Le Kef, set on the side of the hill, comprises numerous mosques and a Turkish* kasbah, *built in 1679 by Mohammed Bey using material pillaged from other monuments. The most striking mosque is that of Sidi Bou Makhlouf, with two domes and an octagonal minaret, flanked by that of El Kebir which has a square minaret. The mosque of El Kebir stands on the site of an older building with a square courtyard surrounded by a portico and a cross-shaped room with niches; the intended use of these is not known.*

70 bottom *Until recently the* kasbah *of Le Kef was inhabited by the army; they have now left and it can be visited. Immediately below it is a small museum, housed in what was originally a basilica and later a mosque. There is another museum in the building that used to house a religious community; it displays mainly pieces relating to the Bedouin culture.*

70-71 *Le Kef rightly bears a name that means "rock": it is located on very uneven ground and there is a difference of nearly 500 feet in height between the lowest and highest parts. Temperatures also vary greatly, passing from the torrid heat of summer to freezing cold in winter. The town is arranged like an amphitheatre and dominates a vast horizon.*

Sidi Bou Said and Monastir, the pearls of the Mediterranean

72 *Many of the homes in Sidi Bou Said have been renovated and rented to foreigners who spend several months a year here, enjoying a tranquillity no longer found elsewhere.*

73 *Perched at the top of a headland on the northern tip of the Gulf of Tunis, the village of Sidi Bou Said owes its beauty to the magic combination of several elements: the air, the fragrant smell of jasmine, the brightly-coloured bougainvillaea, the blue and white houses and a mild climate.*

74   *Before becoming one of the most popular tourist spots in Tunisia, Monastir was one of the holiest places of Islam and before that a strategic base during Caesar's African campaign. Above all it is home to an impressive ribat, a sort of fortified monastery that had special powers for those defending the Muslim faith, especially after Kairouan had been abandoned as a holy city. It is the birthplace of the first President of the Tunisian Republic, Habib Bourguiba and he is buried in the huge mausoleum seen here.*

75 top left   *A detail of the pure gold-covered dome of the mausoleum dedicated to Habib Bourguiba, the first president of the Tunisian Republic and considered the father of the nation.*

75 top right   *Monastir is situated on a picturesque headland and has large parks even in the city centre. In the background is the outline of the Bourguiba mosque, built in 1963 to the design of the mosque of Hamouda Pacha in Tunis.*

75 bottom   *The old town of Monastir has conserved in part its walls, built by Ali Bey in the 18th century, with small square towers, lovely gates, numerous mosques and elegant minarets. Unfortunately most of the medina was demolished to make room for a highly debatable form of tourist attraction and film sets for major international productions.*

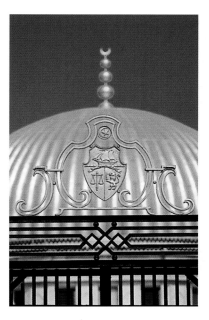

76-77 *The huge ribat of Monastir is a fort commenced in the 9th century with subsequent additions made over the years to the 20th century; viewed from the sea it is a blend of might and elegance. Clearly visible to the fore, the bathing establishments are painted in the traditional blue and white.*

Sfax: minarets and chimneys

78 top *The heart of the town is the* medina, *still completely enclosed within the walls which are of Aghlabid foundation and dark in colour; the maze of alleys and arcades is filled with shops where weavers, blacksmiths, and goldsmith make and sell their wares. The town's most important museum is housed here in a lovely 18th-century palace, the Dar Jallouli, standing right beside the Great Mosque with its three-storey minaret, similar to that of Kairouan. The building has beautiful stucco and carved wood decorations and all the pieces on display are related to folk arts and traditions – costumes, jewellery, furniture and household articles; it has a wonderful section dedicated to calligraphy.*

78 bottom *The main square, Place Hedi Chaker dedicated to a hero of the Independence, is the heart of the new town. On one side stands the Town Hall, embellished with a minaret, the top of which commands splendid views. Inside, a small museum exhibits significant relics from ancient Thaenae.*

79 *The second largest and the most industrial city in Tunisia, modern Sfax has not developed tourism, preferring trade and fishing, especially for sponges. Its vast industrial area processes phosphates and produces oil.*

Mahdia, the cradle of the Fatimids

80 *The town of Mahdia was built in the 10th century on the rocky headland of Cap d'Afrique by Obeid Allah, known as el Mahdi ("one who is guided"), who gave his name to the town. Its strategic and militarily well-defended position was needed by el Mahdi to resist attacks by his enemies, the Kharijites. The Mahdi was a member of the Fatimid family which boasted descent from Fatima, the Prophet's daughter. Mahdia has numerous mosques, some newly-constructed.*

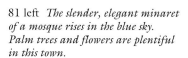

81 left *The slender, elegant minaret of a mosque rises in the blue sky. Palm trees and flowers are plentiful in this town.*

81 centre top *The Skifa el Kahla, or "Dark Passage", is a huge gate-fortress set between polygonal towers, equipped with artillery posts. Originally it was just a tunnel providing passage through the wall, more than 32 feet thick, which prevented access to the town from any external point.*

81 centre bottom *The Borj el Kebir, or "great fortress", is the other important surviving part of the fortifications. Quadrangular in shape, it has a square courtyard, and angular ramparts added in the 18th century; the original fortress was built by the Turks in the 16th century.*

81 top right *The courtyard of the Great Mosque built around 916 by Obeid Allah is elegant and refined but was much tampered with before being renovated and partially reconstructed in the Sixties. The courtyard measures 164 feet by 128 and is surrounded by galleries on three sides. The arches in the narthex, in front of the prayer hall, rest on ancient columns.*

81 bottom right *The medina, once surrounded and defended by the strong walls, blown up by the Spanish of Charles V, extends on the headland towards the sea. Only two fortifications of the walls remain, the Skifa el Kahla and the Borj el Kebir.*

Sousse, the port of Hannibal

82-83 The walls of the Sousse medina (a Unesco Human Heritage center since 1988) surrounding the town are still majestic and perfectly preserved. Inside their circle stands a lighthouse which was part of a coastal communications and defense system that used flags during the day and fires at night for signaling. This city flourished in the 9th century during the Aghlabid period.

83 top The ribat *or* ksar er ribat *is a monastery-fortress, the most important civil construction dating from the first centuries of Arab domain in north Africa. In ancient times a pagan temple and a Christian basilica stood on this site. Near the end of the 8th century the representative of the Abbasid caliph had a fortress built on the Byzantine foundations to protect the port; the work was completed by the Aghlabid emir Ziadet Allah. The* ribat *served both as military barracks and as a monastery: the members of the garrison were considered monks and cavaliers.*

83 centre top The new tourist town has developed north of Avenue Habib Bourguiba. Many hotels have been built along the beach, which attracts mass tourism. Sousse is splendidly positioned for day trips to all the major historic sites in Tunisia.

83 centre bottom The almost square internal courtyard of the ribat *is surrounded by two-storey buildings. On the ground floor an arcade with massive pillars leads to the cells of the monks-cavaliers, the food stores and the stables. A staircase climbs to the first floor and a small museum of ancient inscriptions. The dome above the mihrab is thought to be the first constructed in Tunisia to Oriental designs. The first floor leads to the roof and a terrace protected by crenellated walls, used by the soldiers for defence in the event of an attack. The watch tower also served as a minaret: from the top there is a sweeping view over the* medina, *the new town and the sea.*

83 bottom A courtyard near the Er Reba souq *overlooks the* Kalaout el Koubba, *the "café of the dome" today the Folk museum, an odd 11th-century building topped with a distinctive dome presenting zigzag ridges; its original use is unknown.*

Kairouan, on the edge of the desert

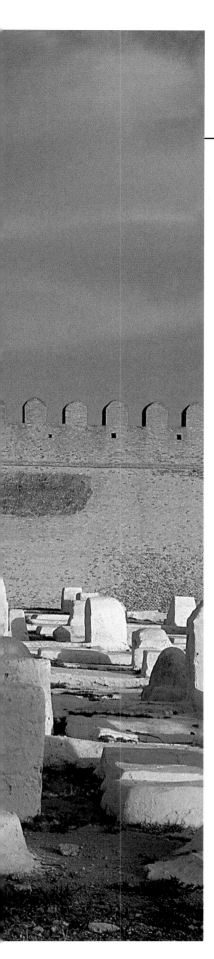

84-85 *The old cemetery has expanded close to the wall of the Great Mosque of Kairouan, one of the most interesting towns in Tunisia and, indeed, in all of north Africa.*

85 left *The entrance to the medina clearly reveals Kairouan's Arab imprint; the town's origins and the Great Mosque make it one of the four most important holy places of Islam together with Mecca, Medina and Jerusalem.*

85 top right *The Great Mosque has a sloping rectangular plan 440 feet by 260. In the centre of the shorter side is the square minaret with two terraces and a dome. A large courtyard paved with slabs of white marble stretches between the prayer hall and the minaret.*

85 centre right *The 240 columns of the prayer hall and arcade around the courtyard come from Roman and Byzantine constructions throughout the country. Each one is different and many have particularly beautiful capitals.*

85 bottom right *The Aghlabid basins are large, open-air reservoirs that collected and purified the water brought by an aqueduct built in the 8th century and now lost.*

86 top *The zaouia of Sidi Abid el-Ghariani is a mausoleum built around the burial-place of this man, considered a saint and who died around 1402. The original building is not large and is entered through a vestibule with a decorated ceiling. The courtyard is surrounded by porticoes and a second level, also porticoed. It leads to the tomb of the saint and other chambers where a small museum of memorial tablets and ancient Koranic calligraphy has been set up.*

86 bottom *The Mosque of the Barber is actually a zaouia, the home of a religious fraternity. The zaouia of Sidi Sahab is built around the tomb of a friend of Mohammed, said to have always carried three hairs of the Prophet's beard around with him; of ancient foundation, it was tampered with in the 17th century when a minaret and a* medersa, *a Koranic school, were added.*

87 top *The porticoed courtyard of the zaouia of Sidi Abid, its arches decorated in black and white, is seen here from the first floor gallery.*

87 bottom *The so-called Mosque of the Barber also has a distinctive large porticoed courtyard.*

88-89 *The zaouia of Sidi Sahab, better known as the Mosque of the Barber, is richly decorated, mainly with tiles that bear geometric and floral motifs, never human figures because of a misinterpreted but always applied ban. Traditional Tunisian ceramics, as still produced today, have particularly bright colours and animated designs. These are found in the second porticoed courtyard, attractively sumptuous, with much stucco-work and dominated by the dome of the sanctuary containing the tomb of Sidi Sahab. The porticoed courtyard is preceded by a vestibule that consists in a square room topped with a dome, finely decorated with stucco-work; this is preceded, in turn, by a small porticoed inner courtyard featuring white marble, applied also to the two windows and a door, clear evidence of late Italian Renaissance influence.*

Jerba,
the island
of Ulysses

90 top left *The Kharijite sect were responsible for the great number of mosques (213) built on Jerba. The picture shows the Jadid or "new" mosque.*

90 centre left *Close to the port, overlooking the sea, is the fort known as Borj el Kebir; built by the Aragonese in the 13th century, it was later extended by the Spanish.*

90 bottom left *All sorts of things are found in the souq of Houmt Suq, from handmade articles to spices.*

90 right *Lateen-sail boats, characteristic of the island, are anchored in the waters around Jerba.*

90-91 *Houmt Suq, a village now become a town with modern districts, is the capital of the island of Jerba. The souq of Jerba is always very crowded and you can find everything there, from the unlikeliest junk to genuine, traditional craftsmanship. The simplest items to buy are sponges, pottery, woollen fabrics and jewellery. A visit to the Museum of Popular Arts and Traditions will give you a good idea of what is worth buying.*

A portrait of the Tunisian People

92 top *Tunisia has a wide variety of traditional costumes, although many are now being abandoned, especially in the cities and by young people who pursue Western models. These costumes survive thanks to folk groups such as these at Metlaoui, a mining town close to Gafsa. The musicians wear a beige* burnous *over a spotless* jellaba *and an unusual green kerchief.*

92 bottom *This is a café on Jerba, but it could be a traditional café anywhere in Tunisia, patronised by locals. Despite the existence of sexual equality, sanctioned by the constitution, only men sit in the cafés. And men smoke the* narghile *although women do smoke it, but not in public. The* narghile *is a sort of pipe in which the smoke passes through a cooled tube before it is inhaled.*

93 *On the island of Jerba the men use boats but the women practise a more primitive form of fishing, wading into the shallow waters found at many points around the island. The area most plentiful in fish, thanks to the currents, is around the Borj Kastil point, the ideal place to try this type of fishing with a rod.*

Fishing,
an ancient art

94 top left *Fishing is also widely practised on the Kerkennah islands which abound with palm trees, essential for the local fishing methods: it is a most productive kind, aided by fixed barriers that incorporate funnel-shaped traps ending in a closed chamber into which the fish swim as the tide ebbs. All is constructed with palm fronds. They also fish from boats with lateen sails, some of the last left in the Mediterranean.*

94 bottom left *In northern Tunisia, at Tabarka and nearby, they fish with more modern means and methods: large motor boats and trawl nets. They have always fished and traded coral, once a prerogative of the Genoese Lomellini family who owned the island opposite the port.*

94 top right *A fishing trawler is anchored in the port of Tabarka while the sailors repair nets on the jetty.*

94 bottom right *Small fishing boats shored on the coast of the Kerkennah islands. These are traditional and used all over the Mediterranean; they have just one mast and a triangular sail.*

95 *An elderly fisherman makes a net in the port of Kelibia. Renowned for being well-protected even when a very strong wind is blowing, it is a refuge for a large fishing fleet; they fish with the* lampara *(boats for night fishing), just as they do in Sicily. Leisure craft can also moor in the port of Kelibia. The coastline is rocky and, as well as fishing, the inhabitants of Kelibia farm grow grapes and produce good wine.*

94

Souqs and bazaars

96-97 *A Sousse craftsman at work in the shop in the* souq. *He makes brass plates and trays using a burin to engrave traditional stories and images or religious inscriptions in Arab script. These are often enamelled in bright colours.*

97 top *These puppets, of clearly Turkish influence, are moved using wires just like the Sicilian "pupi", their close relatives.*

97 centre right *At Hammamet, where this photograph was taken, as elsewhere in Tunisia, the women envelope themselves in a sort of sheet when they go out. Although usually white, it may be another colour, even black. It protects them from indiscreet looks, the dust and the heat, but is a vanishing custom.*

97 bottom right *Kairouan is still the most legendary centre in Tunisia for the traditional production of woven and knotted carpets.*

97 centre left *The blankets of Jerba are famous, even though they are made with larger and coarser woollen yarns than used in Europe. Some may feel rough, but they often feature highly interesting combinations of colour and design.*

98 top left *The most fascinating part of the Tunis* souq *is covered to protect against the summer heat and winter cold. The covered* souq *starts on the right-hand side, looking towards the Great Mosque entrance, below an impressive arch. In this area is the Suq el Attarine (perfumes), the Suq el Koumash (fabrics), the Suq des Femmes (clothing), the Suq et Truk (carpets). Each of these* souqs *lead to others, hidden in a maze of alleyways.*

98 centre left *Buying anything in a shop is often a ritual involving many rules of courtesy for vendor and purchaser alike, such as the offer of a cup of tea by the former and a readiness to bargain in the latter.*

98 bottom left *Carpets are found everywhere but there are, of course, carpets and carpets, just as there are different selling areas. This is the Suq el Leffa, one of the oldest* souqs *in Tunis; here no one will insist with the offer of a carpet unless sure you really want to buy one.*

98 centre right *A shopkeeper sitting at the entrance to his shop is patiently awaiting customers. He is wearing a small, red, cloth fez, named after the town in Morocco.*

98-99 *The* souqs *in the* medina
*of Tunis are divided into guilds, or
rather types of product; gold and
jewellery are found in the Suq des
Orfèvres.*

100-101 *The* souq *of Tozeur, a town
on the edge of the desert, offers a good
selection of carpets, both* kilims *and
knotted, with designs often inspired
by ancient Roman mosaics.*

Ancient roots and noble customs

102 top left *The so-called troglodyte dwellings of Matmata are villages dug by the Berbers of the same name into the friable rock terrain; below, rooms open onto these cylinders sunk into the ground; sometimes there are two levels to provide a granary or store for other necessities. Matmata also* has some marhalas, *small hotels and lodgings created by combining some dwellings; these perhaps give a better understanding of the spatial relationship between access-tunnels, courtyard-craters and cave-rooms or stores than the single dwellings.*

102 bottom left *At Metlaoui, marriage is a cause for celebration also for the children: they dress in white or other colours, tattoo their hands and feet and wear a veil and jewellery as well as hats embroidered with the name of God, Allah.*

102 right *Metlaoui is a mining centre visited by foreigners only for business purposes. Western models have not yet ousted tradition, and marriages are occasions for great popular participation: all the people, men especially, fill the streets, forming noisy processions that last until the small hours.*

103 *Tunisia is a country with a rich variety of costumes. Major differences can still be observed between one place and another, even when situated close together. The women of Matmata, for instance, wear a veil on their heads, a long, white* jellaba *and over this a striped cloth in the colours of the southern lands, fastened with a fibula, just as in ancient Rome.*

104-105 *On the road to Sbeitla, a man in traditional dress with a hood, the ancient woollen* burnus, *lights up a French cigarette watched by a shepherd clothed in the same way.*

106-107 *This Berber bride of Jerba
wears a dress rich in fabric and colour,
plenty of silk and red, embellished with
gold embroidery and jewellery. Her face
is uncovered, unlike the custom of many
villages inland.*

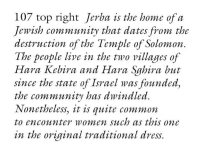

107 top right *Jerba is the home of a Jewish community that dates from the destruction of the Temple of Solomon. The people live in the two villages of Hara Kebira and Hara Sghira but since the state of Israel was founded, the community has dwindled. Nonetheless, it is quite common to encounter women such as this one in the original traditional dress.*

107 bottom right *Another woman of Jerba has chosen to wear white, to enhance her ebony complexion and hands. As well as the fabrics, jewellery is an important item of dress. A manifestation of accumulated wealth, the nomads in particular collect bracelets, anklets and ear-rings that are often very heavy.*

107 top left *The women of Jerba must cover their heads, not the face, which remains visible. Often, however, when they need to free their hands they hold a corner of their head-covering between their teeth.*

107 bottom left *The island of Jerba is in the south and has always had frequent contacts with dark-skinned peoples. You often meet beautiful women of mixed blood who like to dress in contrasting colours such as blue and red.*

The places
of worship

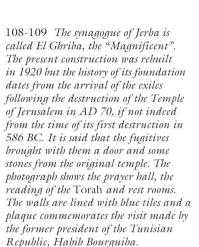

108-109 *The synagogue of Jerba is called El Ghriba, the "Magnificent". The present construction was rebuilt in 1920 but the history of its foundation dates from the arrival of the exiles following the destruction of the Temple of Jerusalem in AD 70, if not indeed from the time of its first destruction in 586 BC. It is said that the fugitives brought with them a door and some stones from the original temple. The photograph shows the prayer hall, the reading of the Torah and rest rooms. The walls are lined with blue tiles and a plaque commemorates the visit made by the former president of the Tunisian Republic, Habib Bourguiba.*

109 top *The prayer hall is dominated by a raised altar used for wedding ceremonies. Jewish visitors are received by a barefoot rabbi who asks them to be seated, places his hands on their heads and blesses them.*

109 centre *The exterior of the synagogue which conserves what is thought to be one of the oldest Torahs in the world; it is the object of pilgrimage in spring, 33 days after Easter. The pilgrimage celebrates the foundation of the synagogue and commemorates the "miracle" of an unknown girl who was suddenly enveloped in flames but who died without a burn mark.*

109 bottom *A funduk has been built beside the synagogue; this two-storey hotel has a large internal porticoed courtyard and is used to accommodate the pilgrims. Many, however, prefer to spend the week in one of the numerous villages along the coast.*

An oasis snatched from the desert

110 top *The swimming pool of the* Jerba Menzel *hotel is one of the most popular. The island was subjected to a savage increase in building development to satisfy tourism, when huge hotels taking 2,500 guests were opened. Now there is a tendency to cut back and promote alternative forms of accommodation, such as old* funduks, *converted to* marhalas, *quaint hotels for visitors who prefer to avoid the crush of the large hotels or holiday villages.*

110 bottom *The* Hotel Abu Nawas *in Gammarth is one of the hundred or more hotels opened on the Tunisian coasts over the last 20 years. In Tunisia the most popular areas with tourists, starting from the north, are: Tabarka, the coasts of Bizerte and Tunis, the Cap Bon peninsula, Nabeul and Hammamet, the beaches of Sousse and Monastir, the coasts of Sfax and Gabès, and the island of Jerba.*

111 top *Port el Kantaoui (the harbour can be seen here) is a luxury holiday complex built in 1979 on the coast of the gulf of Hammamet, in an uninhabited area.*

111 bottom *Port el Kantaoui is ideal for those not attracted by local colour; everything is modern, with excellent restaurants, air conditioning and discos.*

The Roman heritage

112 top *The Capitol, with forum, grand theatre, baths and the Temple of Caelestis, is one of the best examples of the Romanisation of Dougga, the ancient Thugga. Of Punic origin, the town was annexed to Rome in 46 BC by Julius Caesar.*

112 bottom *Bulla Regia, after the death of Massinissa, was the capital of one of the Numidian kingdoms; its ruins occupy a vast area in the hills. Under Roman influence beginning from the 1st century AD, the city prospered until the late 4th century. Then, it began to decline and was abandoned in the 6th century.*

113 *The capitol of Sbeitla is in a remarkable state of conservation. The ancient Sufetula, it was founded by the Romans in the 1st century AD.*

Carthage, the city of the Phoenicians

114 *This curly head escaped the plundering perpetrated after the Arabs destroyed the town. Carthage became a huge field of ruins and for centuries supplied building materials for the expansion of the nearby city of Tunis.*

114-115 *The Roman remains of the city of Carthage, founded in 814 BC by the Phoenicians of Tyre, stand on the point that closes the Gulf of Tunis to the north; in the distance is the peninsula of Kelibia, closing it to the south.*

115 top *This lovely floor is part of the Roman city reconstructed by Caesar and Augustus, capital of the Roman province of Africa from AD 46 onwards. The city experienced another period of splendour as a Christian centre, but then came the Vandals, followed by the Byzantines; the Arabs destroyed it completely in AD 697.*

115 bottom *A lovely Corinthian column is miraculously still standing. As told in school books, Phoenician Carthage prospered rapidly, founding colonies and extending its domain to the western Mediterranean. It fought first with the Greek colony of Syracuse for the possession of Sicily, then with Rome; despite initial success, it had to succumb to Roman power. It was totally destroyed by the Romans in 146 BC, at the end of the third Punic War.*

The long arm
of Rome

116 top *Little remains of the Numidian town of Thougga, as Dougga was known in ancient times, save for the magnificent Mausoleum of Ateban, the only monument in the world to bear motifs of ancient Greece and Egypt, with a spire that is an early form of the Muslim minaret, and Oriental bas-reliefs.*

116-117 *The amphitheatre of El Jem was built by Gordian when from proconsul he was elected emperor in AD 238; it was never completed. El Jem was founded at the time of Caesar with the name of Thysdrus and was a rich north African colony, thanks to the vast cultivations of olives in the area. At the end of the 7th century, the amphitheatre was used as a fortress by the famous Berber queen Kahena in her heroic but unfortunate battle against the Arab invaders.*

117 top *The Capitol of Dougga in central Tunisia is the heart of what is a almost mountain version of Pompei, equally composite and indicative of the life conducted here for almost 600 hundred years spanning the birth of Christ. Dougga is rich in houses, gymnasiums, theatres, circus, forum, baths and places sacred to the gods, and reached the height of its splendour under the Antonines and Septimius Severus. A paved Roman road leads to the Capitol, with the Forum nearby. Other major monuments are the Arch of Alexander Severus, the cisterns, the Temple of Caelestis – the Roman version of the Punic goddess Tanit – and some lovely private houses, such as the House of the Seasons and that of the Trifolium.*

117 bottom *Another view of the El Jem amphitheatre, partially destroyed by a Bey who used explosives to flush out rebels who had taken refuge there. After that episode it served as a stone quarry for the construction of the Arab village. For lovers of numbers the El Jem amphitheatre could hold 35,000 spectators, it measures 485 feet by 400 and the arena is 213 feet long by 121 wide; it is only slightly smaller than the Colosseum in Rome (50,000 spectators, external dimensions 610 feet by 511 and arena of 255 feet by 150).*

118 top *The ruins of Bulla Regia stand on a plateau between Tunis and Ghardimaou. The House of the Hunt is an underground villa built around a patio open at the centre and supported on eight columns; the rooms open onto the patio. The House takes its name from a mosaic now exhibited in the Bardo museum in Tunis.*

118 bottom *A portal provided access to the Thuburbo Majus Baths; this town was founded by the Romans and rebuilt by them in the 4th century with the name of Respublica Felix. The town is especially rich in mosaics, many of which are conserved in Tunis.*

118-119 *Thuburbo Majus was born twice: once when the Romans founded it in 27 BC, and a second time when it was rediscovered by the archaeologist Tissot in 1875; the excavations date from 1912. Octavius Augustus had it built for his veterans, complete with Forum, Capitol, Summer and Winter Baths, Market and several holy places, uncovered in all their glory.*

119 top *The Palace of Amphitrite is actually a temple dedicated to Neptune. The mosaic floor represents Amphitrite on the Centaur with Neptune and winged spirits.*

119 bottom *The principal mosaic of the Palace of Amphitrite is well preserved and visible in all its detail; this is the head of Neptune.*

120-121 *Maktar, the ancient
Mactaris just over 60 miles from Tunis
towards Kairouan, was originally a
Numidian fortress; it became a Roman
colony in AD 180 and was abandoned
after various vicissitudes around the
year 1000.*

121 left *The Trajan arch beside a Punic temple turned into a church and of which but a few shapeless ruins remain. Like Thuburbo Majus, Maktar lived its greatest period of splendour between the 2nd and 3rd centuries.*

121 top right *At Ammedara, the remains of the Byzantine stronghold built under Justinian comprises churches, towers and walls, still an impressive sight.*

121 centre right *The ruins of Utica, about 20 miles from Tunis contain, as well as Punic tombs (the contents are on show in a museum), wide Roman roads, porticoes and lovely houses with marble and mosaic paving.*

121 bottom right *On the road between Le Kef and Gafsa on the border with Algeria, near Haidra, are the ruins of*

the ancient Ammedara; under Augustus this was the winter camp of the III legion, entrusted with the defence of Africa and transported under Vespasian to Teveste where a veteran colony was established. The site at Ammedara is vast and the ruins substantial, starting from the Triumphal Arch of Septimius Severus, dedicated in 195 as indicated by an inscription. The base is flanked by twin columns. In Byzantine times this monument was surrounded by a fort, the remains of which still partially conceal it.

Sbeitla,
the ancient
Sufetula

122-123 *The ruins of the ancient Sufetula, on the site of today's Sbeitla, are huge. Little is known of its history. What is certain is that in 647, date of the first Arab invasion, it was the capital of the Byzantine patrician Gregory, who had declared himself independent and died in battle against the Arabs. The Roman ruins are impressive, with the Capitol and the monumental Antoninius Pius Gate, the columns supporting a well-conserved architrave. The Forum is surrounded by a portico with re-erected columns. At the back are the remains of two of the Capitoline temples, preceded by a peristyle resting on six Corinthian columns. The temples were probably consecrated to the three gods of the Capitol, Jupiter, Juno and Minerva. The area is dotted with forts and Byzantine churches as well as various other fortifications.*

123 top *At Sbeitla, to the right of the road to Tebessa, stands the Triumphal Arch built under the emperor Diocletian. On both sides two columns topped with Corinthian capitals precede rectangular niches flanked by pillars. The Arch has been restored.*

123 centre *Many Byzantine forts are scattered between the road and the river; after these a paved road leads to the monumental Gate of Antoninius Pius, its columns supporting a well-preserved architrave.*

123 bottom *Sufetula flourished under the Severus dynasty. The best-conserved remains of the period include the splendid Capitol, its original design having been based on three separate temples..*

124 *A view from above shows the room on the first floor of the Bardo National Museum in Tunis, filled with extraordinary finds from Roman times.*

124-125 *The Le Bardo district of Tunis is home to the museum of the same name; it has grown up around various mansions and constructions built by the Hafsids and the Beys. At the end of the 19th century it covered an area of many acres and was closed by a wall with ramparts and towers. Many buildings have been knocked down over the years, others have been restored, such as that housing the Bardo National Museum, inaugurated in 1888. The photograph shows one of the main rooms.*

125 top *A statue of Apollo Citharoedus stands out in room VI on the ground floor; here are kept many works from Bulla Regia, mosaics, statues and inscriptions including a mosaic of Perseus and Andromeda, Roman busts and sculptures that adorned a temple dedicated to Apollo.*

125 bottom *The museum has the most important archaeological collection in the Maghreb and is one of the richest in the world in Roman mosaics; it is a treasure chest of artistic finds – this head of Jupiter is but one.*

126 top left *This mosaic depicts Ulysses and the chant of the Sirens. It is conserved in room XVII, as are all those on this page except for that of Virgil.*

126 bottom left *In room XVI, known as that of Virgil, is the mosaic portraying him between the two muses Clio and Melpomene. The mosaic dates from the late 2nd century and was found at Sousse. The papyrus in the poet's hands carries some verses from the Aeneid.*

126 right *This beautiful mosaic features one of the most common artistic motifs: a head of Neptune surrounded by symbols of the sea.*

127 *This mosaic portrait of Diocletian escaped the destruction worked by a succession of invaders arriving on Tunisian soil.*

128 *Sunset on the Kerkennah islands, the palms standing out against a red sky.*

All the pictures are of Alfio Garozzo / White Star except for the following:

Antonio Attini / Archivio White Star: pages 24-25, 122-123, 123 center.

Marcello Bertinetti / Archivio White Star: pages 8, 12-13, 22, 23, 62 top left, 62-63, 65 top, 65 bottom, 74 top left , 90 bottom, 90-91, 92 bottom, 93, 96 center right, 98 bottom, 98-99, 106, 107, 108-109, 109 bottom, 110, 111, 116 top, 117 top, 118 top, 119.

Riccardo Spila/Sime/Sie: pages 82-83.

Map by Cristina Franco